Get Serious About Self-Care

A Lifeline for Career-Driven Women Struggling with Overwhelm, Overwork and Overcommitment

Aisha L. Moore

Copyright © 2025 by Aisha L. Moore.
All Rights Reserved. This book, nor any portion thereof, may be reproduced or used in any manner whatsoever without the expressed written permission of the author except for the use of brief quotations in a book review.

Printed in the United States of America.

ISBN: 979-8-218-39610-7

Edited, Formatted and Published by Empower Her Publishing, LLC
empowerherpublishing.com

Table of Contents

Introduction...v

Part 1
Chapter 1: *Who This Journey Is For*..1

Chapter 2: *Preparing to Get Serious About Self-Care*...........11

Chapter 3: *Understanding Stress and Burnout*....................17

Chapter 4: *Understanding Self-Care*..................................25

Part 2
Introduction to the CARE Framework............................33

Chapter 5: *Clarifying Your Wellness Vision*......................35

Chapter 6: *Cultivating Awareness for Wellness*.................51

Chapter 7: *Reframing Overwhelm*...................................57

Chapter 8: *Reframing Overworking*..................................65

Chapter 9: *How to Avoid Overcommitment*......................73

Chapter 10: *How to Embrace Self-Care*............................77

Acknowledgements..86

Introduction

Are you tired of trying these cute self-care tips but never feeling like your stress is under control?

You've tried regular spa days.
You've tried happy hours with your friends.
You've tried getting a new job.
You've tried a nice vacation.

Yet, you are still stuck in the cycle of chronic stress. If this sounds like you, you are not alone. I know exactly how you feel because I've been there, and my clients have been there too.

Like many self-help books, this one is also based on my journey of going from overwhelmed to overflowing. If you don't care about my story and would rather jump straight to the solutions, feel free to skip to Chapter 1.

When I finished grad school, I had difficulty finding a job. I wasn't having a hard time getting first or even second interviews, but I was not receiving offers. Repeatedly, employers told me that I was overqualified for the companies' entry-level positions. However, I was also not quite senior enough for their senior-level positions. Companies just weren't sure what to do with me. When all was said and done,

Aisha L. Moore

I had nine first and seven second interviews and only received one job offer.

I knew that to continue to excel in my career, I had to solve the problem of being stuck in the middle. I needed my resume to reflect leadership experience, so I worked on improving in this area. I set a personal goal to join a non-profit board within five years. I just pulled the five years out of thin air. I began volunteering with my local nonprofit association for my profession. That seemed like a natural starting point. Soon enough, my volunteer role helped me get to know the board members rather well. After volunteering for one year, they noticed I wasn't shy and had a natural speaking talent. As a result, they asked me to MC their annual meeting and I knocked it out of the park.

Great. There we go—something to show on my leadership resume.

This positive experience resulted in a proposal to join the board and I accepted. I did in one year what I presumed would take five years to achieve.

When annual board elections came around the following year, no one wanted the president's seat. A few of the long-term members convinced me to run. Despite not knowing what was involved, I accepted the opportunity. We did not have employees, so everyone on the board took on tasks to meet our goals.

Progressively, I was asked to join other organizations' boards and initiatives during my four-year tenure as board president. I said yes to every offer because I was interested in the missions. I also said yes to fill my resume gap. I will admit to hogging some of the work, and in hindsight, I should have

Introduction

given more opportunities to other rising stars.

Because of the visibility gained as board president, a former colleague reached out to me when she was looking for a director for a project she was working on. She needed a leader and I had proved that I was one. My plan worked. Not only was I on a board, but I was now on four boards. That leadership gap that caused me career problems before was now nonexistent.

I was only in year four of my five-year plan. I had not begun looking for full-time employment at the next leadership level, but dreamed of being a manager. Now I was hand-picked for a director position. I was so excited about this position! I couldn't believe that my plan actually worked! My excitement was short-lived, though. I accepted the job and cried in my cubicle by the end of the first week.

"Oh my God, I forgot to post that blog!" I was waiting late for edits and fell asleep while waiting. Moments later, my stomach rumbled because I feared getting in trouble or worse, fired. I checked my email and the message I was worried about was not there. However, there were 12 emails requesting other things that my superiors wanted completed by 10 am. Unfortunately, I also needed to be at work at 9:15 am for my first scheduled call. I say scheduled calls because there were plenty of unscheduled calls and texts before that.

I was willing to work in this stressful environment because I was amongst movers and shakers. Thousands of people read our blog and I trained thousands of others. I made it to the White House several times. I felt like I was working for President Obama, although I never met him. I was able to edit speeches for cabinet secretaries. Truly, I felt like this behind-the-scenes big deal.

Aisha L. Moore

Waking up every day at 4 am in a panic about something work-related seemed like part of the job. My days began early and ended around 8 pm. I did paid work for 12 hours, unpaid work for three hours, and commuted at least an hour each way every weekday. I always had my laptop, even while on vacation.

To decompress, I attended the occasional happy hour with friends, got facials every month, and tried to get my nails done bi-weekly. I did not always make it to the nail salon though due to working late. Sadly, I never attended the pre-paid weekly in-office yoga classes, though I could see the yoga class in session from my office.

After being in my director position for two years, I understood our busy and less busy periods. I went full out in June and was looking forward to the first two weeks in July being slower. At the end of June, however, the White House asked my team to produce a video to announce their next executive order. While I was flattered that they called my team, surely the White House must have other resources, I thought. I really needed my two weeks to breathe. My co-worker, who was on a deep sea diving adventure, was our video producer, and I had two days to plan it with her before she would be unreachable. We filmed all day and edited late into the night for a week.

The last day of filming was with Dr. Fauci, one of my public health heroes. Everyone knows who that is now. After that interview, we stopped to get something to eat. I pushed my food around on my plate. I wasn't hungry and felt very nauseous.

The videographer looked at me and said, "How do you work like this all the time?"

Introduction

I replied, "It's not like this all of the time."

As I said it, I knew I was lying.

Shortly after, in August, I celebrated my second wedding anniversary. I was finally ready to make our house a home and a newly renovated kitchen would be the perfect touch. As a budget-conscious person, I decided on Ikea cabinets, which were only on sale until the end of the month.

I showed up at Ikea soon after they opened the day before the sale ended. I walked in and, a store I usually find joy in, seemed strange. It felt hot. The other customers seemed close to me and I was so annoyed. I went to the kitchen section and the store associates told me there was an hour before they could get to me. I wanted to escape. I took note of the exit shortcut.

Then I felt dizzy.

I had not eaten yet so I headed to the food court, but grew impatient with the customers ahead of me. My heart was racing and I wanted to lie down. I thought about going to the bathroom but was afraid I might pass out in there. Instead, I got in my car and went home to lie down.

We were down to just one day to get the cabinets at the discounted price. I asked my husband to go with me the next day. When we arrived, I couldn't get out of the car. I started freaking out.

I sat in the car for two hours and waited. While waiting, I called my sister.

"Hey, sis. What does a panic attack feel like?"

She shared her version and I thought maybe that's what was happening to me.

I went to work the next day, and as I left for lunch, I started to feel faint again. Thankfully, I managed to reach the office manager who called an ambulance.

For the next two months, I woke up every day nauseated. I could pull it together and take the train to work some days. On other days, I'd ask my husband to drive me because I feared passing out on the train. When I made it to work, I'd speak to my officemate, start checking emails, then she'd run to a meeting. By the time she'd make it back, I'd be gone.

The nausea made me lose my appetite. I lost five pounds per week, and eventually, my clothes hung off my frame. I visited the doctor every week to determine what was wrong. At each visit, she asked if I was stressed. I'd always respond, "No more than the average person." As an endocrinologist, she tested my thyroid and glucose levels. Nothing came up as an issue.

Unfortunately, I became increasingly unreliable at work. I did not have the energy to keep up, including travel assignments. Within three months, I was on a few medications that helped me get through the day. As a result, I felt well enough to take a short work trip to Boston. That was a mistake. I was wiped out at the end of each day.

There I was, pushing my food around my plate again and not eating. Then, my body shut down during a team meeting on the day I was to fly back.

I couldn't.

Introduction

My co-worker let me stay at her house for a few days. I then stayed at another friend's house for a day and went to a friend's mom's house for a few more days.

Eventually, my husband had to fly up and accompany me on the plane home. Feeling better, I logged on to work from home the next day.

My team lead suggested, "How about you come back when the doctor clears you to come back to work?"

"What do you mean?" I thought. Typically, a note is required to prevent people from taking advantage of sick leave. In my case, I needed my doctor's approval to work. They worried about me, which allowed me to let go.

My doctor officially put me on short-term disability. It was my permission slip to stay home and stop pushing through. My body showed me how bad it was. The barrier I was putting up to hold it all together was gone. That's when the anxiety became apparent. I didn't know that's what I was experiencing. I did not have that language and understanding at the time.

While on short-term disability, I went to the doctor and lots of specialists to determine what was going on. Outside of doctors' visits, I was in bed and taking the prescribed medicines. I believed that rest was the sole cure. I had no other plans. I didn't know anything about self-care or healing. Each Friday, I seemed to feel better. I might even have left the house on the weekend. But Monday would come around and I would feel sick again. I started to ponder if work was triggering me somehow. I continued to rest and hoped to improve by the following week.

After six weeks, I was not entirely better; however, I also was not financially able to go without a paycheck. At this point, my doctor was stumped and recommended I see a therapist. I made an appointment right away.

During my first therapy appointment, I was diagnosed with generalized anxiety disorder. My assignment for the week was to focus on awareness. That did not seem like a very practical solution. There were another six days that I would have to suffer through just trying to do basic things. I did not know if I would make it to the next appointment.

I knew I wasn't entirely well during that first week back to work—the week between Christmas and New Year's Day. I set a small goal to work and stay there all day. That was it. If I felt faint, I would hide in a friend's office. I just needed to stay.

I went to work, then went home and rested. That was it. With awareness top of mind, I noticed that I needed to make more changes in my life other than work. Out of many things, my home office was very cluttered. I thought that decluttering might help. January 1, 2014, I woke up and started cleaning it up. While organizing, I found a piece of paper I had never seen before.

Oh, God, I Need Thee by **Howard Thurman**

I Need Thy Sense of Time
Always I have an underlying anxiety about things.
Sometimes I am in a hurry to achieve my ends
And am completely without patience.
It is hard for me to realize that some growth is slow, that all processes are not swift.
I cannot always discriminate between what takes time to develop and what can be rushed, because my sense

Introduction

of time is dulled.
I measure things in terms of happenings.
O to understand the meaning of perspective that I may do all things with a profound sense of leisure.

I Need Thy Sense of Order
The confusion of the details of living is sometimes overwhelming.
The little things keep getting in my way providing ready-made excuses for failure to do and be what I know I ought to do and be.
Much time is spent on things that are not very important while significant things are put into an insignificant place in my scheme of order.
I must unscramble my affairs so that my life will become order.
O God, I need Thy sense of order.

I Need Thy Sense of the Future
Teach me to know that life is ever on the side of the future.
Keep alive in me the forward look, the high hope, the onward surge.
Let me not be frozen either by the past or the present.
Grant me, O patient Father, Thy sense of the future without which all life would sicken and die.

After reading this, I fell to the floor crying. Who sent this to me – and when?

Anxiety was in the first line and I was just diagnosed with an anxiety disorder.

The second section discussed order and I found this paper while trying to bring order to one of my spaces.

I was unsure of my future, but the third part made me feel hopeful.

How did this paper come to me at this time? There was an obvious answer, a divine answer.

Howard Thurman is my father's favorite author and my father passed away almost two years before this moment. I was sure this paper was from my father, but I never remembered seeing it before. Everything in this poem was what I truly desired in my heart.

Just a few weeks before, my husband had given me some books and courses on meditation. Though I was not going to work for those six weeks, I was not genuinely relaxed. He noticed my breathing was frequently shallow and my mind was always busy. He gave me two Howard Thurman books and access to an online Meditation 101 class for Christmas.

The message was clear. I was to use this prayer as an anchor for my life.

I thought about each part of the prayer and how it applied to my life:

I need thy sense of time.

I am always late. I have no idea how to get to places on time. I barely make it to work on time every day. I am always running for the train. I tell my friends I am close when I haven't even left the house. I procrastinate on everything on my plate, even though it is full and overflowing. I have always been this way. I am just wired this way. I have an anxiety disorder.

I need thy sense of order.

Introduction

My spaces at work and home could be clearer. I have lost my work key card many times and can never find my keys when I walk out the door. I double-book myself for things. All my thoughts are on random sticky notes and in no particular order. I have multiples of many things because I misplace things all the time.

I need thy sense of the future.

I just got demoted from my position. I don't even know if I have the energy to work full-time at this point. I don't know what my life looks like going forward. This job that was a gift turned into a nightmare. What's next?

Instead of lying in bed for the next few days, I dug deeper into the situation. I realized that rest would never be enough if I did not make changes. This prayer helped me see the exact list of changes I needed to make.

I didn't realize how extreme the stress was and how it was affecting me personally. I thought my job was the sole problem and it was not. I was not aware of many of the symptoms of stress in the body, nor was I aware of the psychological symptoms of anxiety. I was also unaware of the limits of my capacity as a human. Like many black women, I was trying to be a superwoman.

What I was aware of, however, was that if work was the problem, then six weeks off should have been the solution. It was not. The solution was actually to make changes that would decrease my stress. I didn't know at the time that what I needed was *transformation.*

No amount of rest was going to help me have a healthy relationship with work.

No amount of rest was going to get me to a daily stress management routine.

No amount of rest was going to help me create and maintain healthy boundaries.

No amount of rest was going to create a robust support system.

Now I was aware, really aware.

This book shares the lessons that I used to go from six weeks of short-term disability, returning to work, getting demoted from my job, starting therapy, and being on five medications to in just 90 days transforming into a completely different person. That wowed both my therapist and my primary care physician and they wanted to know exactly what I was doing.

And the answer was: **I got serious about self-care**.

Then, 18 months later, I was promoted past the director position that I previously had.

My performance review showed that all the work I had been putting in with self-care was reaping benefits for me both personally and professionally. Now, ten years later, I'm still strong.

I have strong friendships and self-care has saved my marriage.

I have great financial habits and a positive net worth.

When we get serious about self-care, it's not a short-term solution. It's a long-term solution and a way of life. We will be healthier and wealthier in a myriad of ways. I cannot wait for

Introduction

you to finish this book and implement what you discover within its pages.

Chapter 1, "**Who This Journey Is For,**" sets the stage by identifying the audience who will benefit most from *Get Serious About Self-Care*. Whether you're feeling overwhelmed, overworked, or simply looking for a roadmap to prioritize yourself, this book provides the tools to transform how you approach self-care. You'll gain clarity on how this journey can help you achieve a balanced and fulfilled life

Chapter 2, "**Preparing To Get Serious About Self-Care,**" introduces the idea that we all have a wake-up call that prompts us to take self-care seriously. Before diving in, the chapter outlines five key agreements that will help guide this journey. These agreements set the stage for a sustainable, meaningful self-care transformation.

Chapter 3, "**Understanding Stress and Burnout,**" explores the evolutionary purpose of stress and its modern-day manifestations. It explains the official definition of stress, the medical definition of burnout, and how to assess when burnout is occurring. You'll also learn how to recognize early signs of burnout using the personal craziness index, helping you take action before stress escalates into burnout.

Chapter 4, "**Understanding Self-Care,**" explores the superficial portrayal of self-care on social media and why it leads to rejection by some. It redefines self-care beyond indulgence, offering a deeper, more meaningful perspective. The chapter breaks down a clear definition and compares it with Audre Lorde's powerful view of self-care as essential for self-preservation.

Sometimes, we read a book that changes our lives just by reading the concepts. Rest assured, if you read and implement the suggestions in this book, you will be transformed forever.

If you struggle with accountability, you can also get coaching to help you make this transformation a reality. I have successfully coached hundreds of people on this system.

Congratulations on your first day of getting serious about self-care!

Chapter 1
Who This Journey Is For

This book is for women looking for strategies to help them overcome mental roadblocks that keep them overwhelmed, overworked, and overcommitted. The strategies in this book will help you use self-care tools, many of which you already have access to, to reduce your stress and, in turn, find a rhythm.

Moreover, if your goal is to excel in your career while maintaining low stress levels and having time for yourself, friends, and family, this book is for you.

When you finish reading this book, you will be well on the path to mastering yourself and having a life well lived. You'll be in control of your time; have the skills to plan and prioritize your life so that you are well rested; and have fun, fulfilling activities that you participate in when you're not working while making much better use of your free time to benefit your health and well-being. You'll have a clearer sense of what's important to you.

Here are a few milestones I hope you will achieve after reading this book:

1. You will have discerningly identified at least one pivotal area of your life that you are eager to cultivate, leading to profound well-being, unburdened ease, and serene peace.
2. You will also possess a vivid and inspiring vision of your extraordinary new life, with self-care solidly anchoring its foundation.
3. You will pinpoint the distinct factors that elevate your stress levels.
4. You will have thoughtfully crafted a revitalizing new schedule that prioritizes self-care and seamlessly integrates into your vibrant life.
5. You will have completed a transformative self-care plan.
6. You will have thoughtfully identified three invaluable individuals for your unwavering support system.

As a career-driven woman who has reached that coveted senior-level position, you've experienced firsthand how stressful these positions can be. However, you did not have the resources to prepare for the stress ahead. Because you didn't prepare for the stress ahead, you've taken on stressful jobs that make you cry at your computer. You have started to experience physical symptoms of stress and burnout, and it is not convenient for you to focus on your wellness.

This book is a solution for continuing the career path you've dreamed about *and* accomplishing your other dreams, including excellent health and wellness.

WHY YOU MIGHT HAVE PICKED UP THIS BOOK
When you are career-driven, high levels of stress are an issue for you in a way that isn't for other people. When you are career-focused, you pay close attention to the people in

positions above you. You formally and informally document how they have gotten ahead and attempt to do the same. You also witness some negative consequences of being career-focused but accept that it is just how the game is played. It's the game you signed up for and agreed to play by the current rules. Here are three rules that you need to reconsider:

Successful Women Work A Lot
I received my first roadmap to being a successful, career-focused woman at my first internship. When I heard, "What do you want for dinner?", I knew we were staying there until 11 pm. We would have probably stayed longer, but 11 was the last train home to my boss' suburban home. I noticed that the most respected people in the company always stayed late and came in on weekends. I did the same, although I only made one-third of their salary.

Fast forward to my first job after grad school. Within the first month of working there, I came in on a Sunday to prepare for a Monday event. My boss, who usually worked remotely, was also there when I arrived. As we were working, she was on the phone with another colleague and said, "Aisha is here too. She's a keeper."

I learned that working a lot was favorable in the eyes of managers and directors, though it rarely translated to a bonus or a better raise. My supervisor rewarded me with praise and that was enough for me.

Successful Women Look Busy
The next thing I learned about being a career-focused woman is that we must perform busyness. One colleague's regular schedule was arriving at the office at 7 am and leaving at 4 pm to pick up her kids. Many people talked about how she always left early, even though she technically worked the same amount of hours as everyone else. She was probably

more productive in those first few hours than those who came in and immediately went for coffee. Unfortunately, because her early mornings were not visible, she did not get the same respect as everyone else who worked just as hard as her but worked later.

I learned that if our hard work is invisible to others, it doesn't count. We have to talk about how overworked we are and how hard we work. Our desk has to be messy. But is it real? Truthfully, many of those late nights and weekends happened because I was distracted and not as productive as possible during the day.

I was busy at work and trying to grow in my leadership positions outside of work. I volunteered for all of the meetings and committees. While this did lead to several opportunities, it also eventually led to me taking on too much responsibility. Ultimately, I stepped down from being "Madame President," as one of my mentors called me. I was genuinely interested in the causes I served, but serving one was enough. When I got to number four, it had a performance gap aspect.

I challenge you to consider how many things you need to do. As high-achieving women, we may overperform and have many commitments that lead us to neglect self-care. We don't have time to think, for anything to go wrong, or to make mistakes. When our career is our number one focus, it leads to being completely overwhelmed with a platinum membership card for "Team Doing Too Much".

Successful Women Do Not Set Limits
Women who are career-oriented, especially those who are salaried, have a hard time setting limits. Oxford Dictionary defines a limit as "a point or level beyond which something does not or may not extend or pass." Business News Daily

Who This Journey Is For

states, "A salaried employee gets paid a set amount based on an agreed-upon annual salary based on a 40-hour workweek." However, somehow, no matter how many hours we work, we still earn the same amount. Most salaried employees expect to work more than 40 hours but also expect the salary to reflect that. Eventually, we accept that working 60-80 hours per week comes with the territory.

The expectation of performing our value with no limits on work hours creates a recipe for overworking. It also alludes to the belief that anything that does not contribute to growing our career is not worth spending time on. Therefore, we may not cultivate hobbies and are likely to skip out on our exercise time to finish up "just a few emails". Even if we stop working, we feel guilty for meeting with friends, binge-watching a show, or even doing laundry.

When new opportunities arise, we do not set limits. Our hard work has paid off and we are sought after for our skills and talents. We say yes to every opportunity presented because, although we crave free time, we make our free time available to others. Then, we feel overwhelmed and cannot figure out why. We don't protect our free time. We confuse not having a scheduled activity with being free to work.

Reframing the Rules

Although this roadmap to success led to high stress, I did not think to learn anything about stress prevention, alleviation, or management. I followed the blueprint to greater titles, salary, recognition, and subsequently, burnout. That is why I highly encourage you to think about this differently if you are going to reduce your stress levels. Take each one of these things and flip it.

Unskillful Belief: Successful women work long hours.

Skillful Belief: Successful women do not overextend themselves.

Unskillful Belief: Successful women look busy.
Skillful Belief: Successful women choose wisely where they want to make an impact.

Unskillful Belief: Successful women do not set limits.
Skillful Belief: Successful women protect their time.

When your job environment is stressful, you should not accept it until you can no longer absorb it. You will fall apart like I did and end up on short-term disability. Fight back against stress and do something about it every single day.

WHY YOU ARE AFRAID TO GET SERIOUS ABOUT SELF-CARE
You might be thinking, "Aisha, I am not afraid."

Then why haven't you put yourself first yet? Not even a baby step. You must be afraid of something.

You Are Afraid You Don't Deserve It
Most of us have had these thoughts:

- I have a salaried job. I have more flexibility to take my mother to the doctor than other family members.
- I do not have kids. I can stay at work later than others.
- I have pretty good life circumstances compared to others. Being exhausted is not a reason to take a break from my advocacy work.

Thoughts like these indicate that taking on more than your fair share of responsibilities is okay. These statements also signal that you believe that you have to push through no matter what. Ultimately, you believe self-care is something you earn. You must do something noteworthy or of merit to feel worthy enough to take time out for self-care.

I want you to consider that we're all human beings. Our bodies, minds, and emotions need maintenance. Therefore, no matter where we are in life, we need self-care. Don't be afraid to carve out time for self-care. Don't self-sabotage yourself out of a self-care routine by thinking there's not enough going on in your life to warrant having a daily self-care practice.

I see this mindset play out with therapy. I was always a fan of treatment; I just never went because I had not experienced a crisis or mental health challenge that I thought warranted it. I did not know that therapy could be used for maintenance to keep my mental wellness in check. I thought I had to have a severe problem. You can feel the same about putting yourself first when it comes to self-care. Instead, you sadly wait until you cannot function before you decide to put yourself first.

You Are Afraid Of Putting Others Last
I get it - you might be afraid of putting yourself first if you feel there are negative consequences to putting your wellness above others' wants and needs. You may think of yourself as the person on the back burner, last on your list, or not even on the list at all. You do things for everybody and neglect yourself.

Inherently, when you begin to talk about putting yourself first, the people at the top of the list become nervous. They assume you are pulling back from meeting their needs and may discourage you from changing. They may even go so far as to make you feel guilty about putting yourself first. They do this because they fear you will start treating them as you currently treat yourself. They are afraid they are going to the bottom of the list where you were. They see how you neglect yourself and are so scared they will get that same treatment.

You make their fears your own.

The reality is that when you are in the first position, they only shift down one. The previous number one spot only goes down to second, but they fear they will enter the last slot. They are afraid of being put on the back burner.

The other truth they don't realize is that they stand to gain much more when you are in first place. When you are in last place, you show up for others exhausted, irritable, and stressed. You might even be prone to flaking on them. When you embrace self-care, on the other hand, you show up more energized and creative. Imagine how happy your children, partners, or friends will be when they have your full, undivided, and pleasant attention. They would love it, right?

Personally, I know my father would have loved it when I was his caregiver. Unfortunately, though, I was constantly tired and had no bandwidth for his special requests. He would take a long time to get to the table when dinner was ready. By the time he got there, the food was cold, and he would complain - although he did have a microwave for easy reheating. I was short with him in my responses. I remember shouting, "Man, if you don't eat this food at this temperature! I am not reheating this!" If I had embraced self-care, maybe I would have been more graceful.

You Are Afraid Your Success Will Stall
Burnout is more likely to ruin your success than getting serious about self-care. When you are doing too much, your mental and physical health may decline, causing you to stop being great at your job.

Who This Journey Is For

You are already an overachiever and that will not change anytime soon. It's who you are. You are never going to become an underachiever. When you get serious about self-care, you will determine how much time and effort you need to put in to get the desired results. You put in extra hours and take on additional projects to secure your success at work. Realistically, it takes a lot less work than you realize to get serious about self-care. Throughout my journey of being serious about self-care, I celebrate that I am doing less each year. I do less and less each year and still receive stellar performance reviews and above-average raises at work.

While writing this book, I was dealing with a new mental health issue that made it challenging to work at total capacity. I started two new projects and the timing could not have been any worse. I used much sick time and wasn't my usual go-getter self. I did just enough work to get by. There were even a few times I had to pull out of engagements.

To be honest, the last thing I expected was to get a promotion. When I announced that I was leaving my previous role, the colleagues and clients I served while I was dealing with my mental health shared that they thought I was irreplaceable. They had not experienced me at 100% capacity, yet they valued what I had to contribute. They unknowingly experienced that I took the best care of myself so they could still benefit from my talents.

When you do this gradually, most people will not notice that you're working less. What will be noticeable, however, is that with adequate rest, exercise, nutrition, and stress management, you will show up as the team's most focused, engaged, and creative member. You have overdone it for so long that you have a considerable success credit line to cash in. More importantly, those attributes will also be available to the people you care about most.

Chapter 2
Preparing to Get Serious About Self-Care

A few years ago, I was working on growing my coaching business. I hired a coach who asked me, "What's going on right before people want to work with you?" I realized that all of my clients have had a wake-up call. For several clients, this involves losing someone they love, going to the funeral, and hearing their eulogy. For others, it was going to the emergency room for a panic attack.

It is usually a life-altering wake-up call that leads one to pick up a book like this. Wake-up calls motivate us to look for solutions. We have to heed that wake-up call. To get the most out of this book, you need a strong desire to create a different kind of life—one with much lower stress levels and greater alignment. You have to fully commit to what you desire. This is not the time to go halfway. This process is designed for you to overhaul your visions, your thinking, and so much more. You have to be all in.

Getting serious about self-care has a few requirements. You must try new things that might make you uncomfortable or unworthy. You must also take your time and avoid taking on too much at once. In some instances, pairing self-care with professional help may be necessary for the best outcomes.

In short, you have to move differently. That can feel risky, especially for women. If it were easy, you wouldn't have needed a wake-up call to inspire you to change. You may imagine losing relationships or getting fired if you change to support your wellness. The truth is, burnout can lead to those same outcomes.

From my journey and the journeys of others, I know that we're better off after making these changes. I have countless stories of women who've found the courage to stop accepting mediocrity, changed their workplaces, built more robust support systems, and found greater satisfaction in how they spend their time.

AGREE TO TRY IT ON

When I went shopping for my wedding dress, there was a dress in the window that I wasn't particularly fond of. I immediately said, "Wow, that's ugly." I proceeded into the store and tried on a few dresses. Nothing was entirely right. The salesperson brought me the very dress I had dismissed and I expressed my hesitation. Still, she insisted I try it on. I did—and lo and behold, it was *the* dress! I looked amazing. To top it off, I could zip off the bottom and turn it into a party dress. It had more benefits than I realized and I would have never known if I hadn't tried it on.

Each day, when we open our phones and browse social media, articles tell us we're doing something wrong. "If you've been baking a cake like this, you're doing it wrong." When we click the link, we might discover a fantastic new way to bake a cake that makes it more moist. However, we probably have a tried-and-true, memorized, and easy-to-use recipe. To start doing it the new way, we'd have to be more intentional. It may seem harder at first because we have to put thought into it. We want a more moist cake, but is the effort worth it?

Similarly, the same is true in this process of learning and implementing effective self-care. You'll learn many things, but you must intentionally incorporate them. It takes more work, but is it worth it when you sleep well, have more than enough energy, have a reasonable work schedule, and have more fulfilling relationships? Is it worth it to be in control of your life?

There will be strategies that seem like a great fit and others that won't. I ask that you try everything to see if it works for you. You might be surprised. The worst that could happen is taking it off and leaving it behind.

AGREE TO GET THROUGH YOUR DISCOMFORT
Some steps to establishing a healthy self-care regimen will make you feel uncomfortable. Discomfort is probable, but not pain or danger. You might feel ashamed that you didn't know certain things, ashamed of not being kind to yourself in the past, or ashamed of drinking the corporate Kool-Aid. You may even discover you can't relate to specific friends or family anymore.

Ultimately, you'll become so excited about your changes that you'll want to tell everyone. But I encourage you to move in silence, like the "G" in lasagna. When you share your process with those not on the same journey, they'll often meet you with their fears. They'll tell you why it's unrealistic and won't work. You don't need those thoughts in your head. If you stick with this, they'll notice the changes and eventually ask you how you did it. That'll be your moment to share.

It's not just others who may be harmful in this process; your inner negativity bias will also show up. Research shows that "across an array of psychological situations and tasks, adults tend to learn from and use negative information far more than positive information." You've been using the same patterns for so long that, although they aren't working and don't get you the desired results, you continue them because they're familiar. Familiarity is comfy, like a fluffy robe in winter. You feel very comfortable wearing the robe of stress. When you take that robe off, you might feel exposed and vulnerable. As you try to do things differently, you'll feel discomfort because it's unfamiliar. You must get comfortable with being uncomfortable to see the results. If you abandon things too soon, you'll never see the benefits. You have to push through; eventually, feeling good will feel more comfortable than feeling bad. Your stress tolerance will decrease to the point where you can't imagine how you ever spent more than a day in high-stress situations.

AGREE TO EMBRACE YOUR WORTHINESS
Earlier in the book, I mentioned that you might have picked this book up because you don't feel you deserve self-care.

One of the reasons I had difficulty with self-care early on is that I have a heart for service. My father instilled this in me early. When he would drop me off for the school bus, he'd say, "Make a difference."

In my professional life, I did just that. My passion for the field drove me. I was always so grateful to give my time and energy to others, especially those who didn't have what I had. You might ask yourself, "Who am I to have a life without stress when everyone else is stressed?" or "Why do I deserve this?"

This line of thinking is even more pervasive in the helping professions like healthcare, public health, and social work. There was a time I was doing advocacy for people with HIV.

They struggled for fundamental rights like medications and housing. One of the participants coincidentally lived near me. As we were leaving a meeting one day, I started walking to the train to make my way home and I assumed she was too. Instead, she began walking in the other direction. I mentioned heading to the train, and she said, "Oh, I don't take the train; I take the bus." It was 8:30 p.m., and while the train would take 45 minutes if everything aligned perfectly, her bus commute would probably take at least two hours. I offered to pay for her train fare, but she declined.

That moment illuminated my privilege and social advantages. I internalized it and similar moments, concluding that I wasn't worthy of rest. As a result, when I was tired, I'd push through because I didn't feel like my life was "bad enough" to deserve rest. Knowing that we can sit behind, not worrying about rent or groceries while others struggle, can make us uneasy. It may feel selfish to rest while others are in need.

I didn't realize I was thinking this way until my first business coach gave me a book, *Manifest Your Destiny*, by Wayne Dyer. The "Honoring Your Worthiness To Receive" chapter made me realize I didn't feel worthy of rest, sleep, or downtime. He explains that when we don't feel worthy of basic things, we might label self-care as selfish. It's connected to why taking care of ourselves makes us feel guilty. We feel like we don't deserve peace and calm in our lives. We'll continue to reject them unless we believe we're worthy of these things. They will never become part of our way of life. We can't be afraid to want and accept what we desire for our health and wellness.
Feelings of unworthiness may arise during this process. Let's not ignore or stuff them away. Instead, observe them, investigate them, and nurture that part of yourself.

AGREE TO SEEK PROFESSIONAL HELP IF NEEDED
To practice effective self-care, you must accurately assess what

is happening. Professionals can help you gain clarity to determine the right combination of professional help and self-care. I started my journey by seeking professional help from a primary care doctor and a therapist. The two of them confirmed that what I was experiencing was anxiety. Their guidance allowed me to reach a place of basic stability, which gave me the energy and focus to take self-care seriously. It was only after following their professional recommendations that I was able to build my self-care plan around managing anxiety, not just pampering.

Professional help is especially essential if you're exhibiting physical signs of stress. You may need medication and other therapies as part of your plan. While it's not a requirement, many of my clients have worked with a therapist before starting our work together. Therapy is a fantastic tool for exploring the root causes of stress. It helped me understand my symptoms and gave me the bandwidth to identify my stressors and triggers and how best to avoid or manage them. It illuminated the path for my self-care journey.

AGREE TO ADDRESS ONE THING AT A TIME
As a high achiever, you may want to fix everything at once to "get on with life". However, you'll succeed more by focusing on one area at a time. When you take on too much, it can replicate the same patterns that lead to overwhelm. In later chapters, we'll identify what to work on and work through consecutively.

Focusing is crucial to avoid moving in too many new directions at once. You don't have to make all your choices immediately and you can only be serious about self-care when you focus on one thing at a time.

Chapter 3
Understanding Stress and Burnout

Stress is a natural part of life but can wreak havoc on our minds and bodies when unmanaged. While stress was initially meant to protect us from physical danger, the stress we face today often comes from everyday pressures — work deadlines, financial worries, or relationships. These stressors might not seem life-threatening, but they still activate our body's response system, leaving lasting impacts.

In my life, I ignored many signs of stress for far too long. I thought my headaches were due to dehydration or that my irritability was just a lack of sleep. I didn't realize that my body was sending me clear signals that something was wrong. I was constantly tired, losing my appetite, and snapping at people I cared about. All these were ways my body communicated that I needed to slow down. Looking back, I wish I had recognized these signs for what they were — stress showing up in my body.

This section will define stress, explore the clinical signs of burnout, and guide us in recognizing the behaviors that indicate burnout may be approaching. By recognizing these signals early, we can take the necessary steps to manage stress before it escalates.

STRESS EXPLAINED
Stress is the body's response to a perceived threat or challenge—whether physical, emotional, or psychological. When we encounter stressful situations, our bodies release hormones like cortisol and adrenaline, which prepare us to respond quickly. While this can be helpful in short bursts, chronic stress can overwhelm our system. This prolonged state of stress leads to physical symptoms because our bodies are not meant to stay in a heightened state of alert. As a result, stress manifests physically—through headaches, muscle tension, digestive issues, or sleep disturbances—alerting us that something in our environment or routine needs to change.

To help you understand how stress may manifest in your life, I've included a chart outlining ten typical signs of stress on the body. Recognizing these signs early can help you take action before stress leads to burnout.

10 SIGNS OF STRESS ON THE BODY

Headaches: Stress can lead to muscle tension and constriction of blood vessels, resulting in headaches.
Fatigue: Chronic stress can disrupt sleep patterns, leading to persistent fatigue and low energy levels.
Muscle tension: Stress triggers the body's "fight or flight" response, causing muscles to tense up, potentially leading to pain or discomfort.
Digestive issues: Stress can affect digestion by altering blood flow and hormone levels, contributing to problems like indigestion or irritable bowel syndrome.
Increased heart rate: Stress activates the release of stress hormones, which can elevate heart rate and blood pressure.
Chest pain: Stress-induced muscle tension and increased heart rate can lead to chest discomfort or tightness.
Weakened immune system: Prolonged stress suppresses immune function, making the body more susceptible to infections and illnesses.
Skin problems: Stress can exacerbate skin conditions like acne, eczema, or psoriasis due to its impact on hormone levels.
Weight changes: Stress might lead to overeating or loss of appetite, resulting in weight gain or loss.
Mood changes: Stress can trigger anxiety, irritability, mood swings, or even depression due to its effects on neurotransmitters in the brain.

BURNOUT: WHAT TO WATCH FOR

Stress and burnout are related but very distinct conditions. We often use burnout casually, but it is typically associated with chronic and prolonged exposure to high levels of stress. It is usually linked to ongoing work-related stressors, such as an overwhelming workload, lack of control, and feeling stuck in a situation.

Burnout is now officially recognized as a legitimate medical condition. As a medical condition, it is no longer seen as just a feeling or temporary phase — it is classified in medical systems with a formal diagnosis. It is described as a state of vital exhaustion and includes three main components:

Feeling drained: You know that bone-deep exhaustion that makes you feel like you can't even? That's the first part of burnout. It's more than just regular tiredness; it can also come with headaches and muscle aches.

Getting super cynical: Burnout makes you hate your job, co-workers, and maybe even yourself. It's like you are emotionally detached from work, which doesn't do any favors for your productivity or job satisfaction.

Losing your professional mojo: Burnout can mess with your confidence and make you doubt your skills. For women, who often juggle work and family responsibilities, this can be extra tough because it piles on top of other challenges you face in the workplace.

It might not sound like a big deal, but it's a game-changer. With this official diagnosis code, doctors can more easily spot burnout and provide the right help and resources. Plus, it could help chip away at the stigma around burnout, making it less scary for you to seek help.

PREDICTING BURNOUT BEFORE IT ESCALATES

After a speaking engagement, one of the attendees approached me and shared that what I presented resonated with her. She asked if I knew about the Personal Craziness Index (PCI). I researched it later and found that the tool was adapted for measuring our level of burnout and predicting it before it becomes a problem.

We often understand that stress is an inevitable part of life and that we will always encounter it. Nevertheless, where do we draw the line between well-managed stress and burnout? The Personal Craziness Index can help determine that. It assists in recognizing how stress manifests in your routine behaviors, allowing you to identify stress before it becomes evident as physical symptoms.

The PCI is based on studies of addictions and the 12-step recovery programs. There are early indicators you can pay attention to that signal whether you may be heading toward burnout. Dr. Carns, the creator of the PCI, notes that craziness initially appears in simple, routine behaviors that support lifestyle balance.

He explains, "We can get caught up in major issues and overlook that our checking account is overdrawn. If our checking account is overdrawn, we are likely out of socks, too, because we haven't done our laundry. If this pattern persists, there's a risk that our lives will also become emotionally bankrupt—regardless of the big issues at hand."

As high achievers, people around us highlight our successes and achievements. However, they might not see that we can't find our keys, are always rushing, have a sink full of dirty dishes, or hide a stain on our shirt with a scarf.

I often fell into the classic trap of saying, "I'll get gas in the morning!" Not getting gas the day before usually triggered a chain reaction of stress the next day. First, I searched for my keys and chastised myself because I did not put them in my purse. Then I remembered the gas light was on and hoped I would reach my destination. This caused me to be late and added to my mental clutter on the way to work. This repeated cycle of anxiety depleted me by the time I reached my desk. Amidst the constant chaos, I overlooked simple solutions like putting my keys on a hook and not letting the gas tank get low.

Everyone experiences personal craziness occasionally, but it's a sign of stress and overwhelm when it occurs repeatedly. The chaos is the precursor to headaches, stomachaches, and irritability. Personal craziness becomes an issue because we are so focused on our work and community mission that we overlook personal problems. The PCI helps us monitor when we stop doing things that support our lifestyle balance. Out of the 12 lifestyle areas, the PCI suggests focusing on ten that are relevant to most people:

1. Physical Health
2. Transportation
3. Environment
4. Work
5. Interests
6. Social Life
7. Family/Significant Others
8. Finances
9. Spiritual Life and Personal Reflection
10. Symptom Behaviors

These signs of burnout will occur in patterns across different areas of our lives. Everyone's expression of "craziness" will be unique. For instance, you may determine walking five days a week in the morning supports your lifestyle balance. You will still function optimally if you skip and adjust to walking a few days in the evening. Suppose you drop down to four–that is still solidly stable. If you get down to two days, however, and that happens week after week, then your lifestyle will not be supported. That means you are at risk of burnout, according to the PCI.

Now that you understand the concept, here is how you use the index. Identify seven habits that support daily lifestyle balance. They should be tiny things. At the end of each day, mark off each thing not accomplished. At the end of seven days, tally up the score, and it will fall between 0 and 49.

This is how to interpret the score:

0-9 OPTIMUM HEALTH
Maintains clear priorities, aligns behavior with values, is balanced, supportive, and creative, and quickly resolves crises.

10-19 STABLE SOLIDLY
Understands personal limits, maintains boundaries, feels competent and supported, and handles crises well.

20-29 MEDIUM RISK
Often feels rushed, struggles with time management, and is vulnerable to slipping into old habits with little emotional margin.

30-39 HIGH RISK
Living in extremes, feels irresponsible, has strained relationships, and frequently fails to follow through on commitments.

40-49 VERY HIGH RISK
Engages in self-destructive behavior, overly focused on projects, blames others for failures, and struggles with timely productivity.

When I learned about this system, I had already practiced daily self-care for about a year, so my score was low. After reviewing the rubric, I realized that I had been living between 30 and 39 for a long time before implementing self-care, which led to my burnout. As high achievers, we should do this index regularly to monitor our burnout levels.

Chapter 4
Understanding Self-Care

At the beginning of my journey, I didn't know it had a name. It was simply the things I did to ensure I made it to the next therapy appointment. After 90 days of doing things to make myself feel better, I did, in fact, feel a lot better. My primary care physician and my therapist were surprised at how quickly I started to recover. They thought it would be at least 18 months. When I told them what I was doing, they identified my new habits as *self-care*.

It was 2014, four years into Instagram's existence; therefore, it was not my first time hearing the term self-care. Much of what I was doing did not resemble anything under the hashtag #treatyoself, which people use to tag self-care content.

It wasn't easy.
It wasn't pretty.
It wasn't pampering.
It wasn't an occasional thing.
It wasn't expensive.

I was inspired to start blogging and speaking about self-care from my experience to include a different perspective.

In 2017, the brilliant, award-winning author and commentator

Aisha L. Moore

Melissa Harris-Perry penned an extensive essay in Elle Magazine titled "How #SquadCare Saved My Life". I wasn't expecting to see this quote in it:

"I refuse to accept that self-care is necessary for health and well-being." -Melissa Harris-Perry

Using the hashtag in the article's title signals she was talking about the aesthetic version of self-care we see online. Although she touches on bell hooks and Ella Baker's take on self-care, she argues that "self-care encourages women to rely solely on themselves rather than to make demands on anyone or anything else." Nothing could be further from the truth. Women can do both. On therapy days, I did my usual self-care routine and attended therapy, followed by lunch with my friend, Aziza. In one day, there was self-care and professional care immediately followed by #SquadCare.

In reality, self-care is the training ground where I honed my ability to be a better squad member. My commitment to self-care improved many people's lives—ask my husband, my book club members, and everyone I work with. I am a better person and have the bandwidth to truly serve others now because I have learned how to take better care of myself. There is no #SquadCare without self-care.

I understand taking issue with the version of self-care sold to us as a luxury good. People with more resources, privilege, and free time have more access to the commodified version. Dr. Harris-Perry revealed that some people have an issue with the concept in its most basic terms. I believe that self-care is essential for health and well-being. Dr. Harris-Perry and I will have to agree to disagree.

Understanding Self-Care

DEFINING SELF-CARE

Given the controversial nature of the term, I want to share a definition that we will use throughout this book.

Self-care is a set of personal practices that build resilience and support us feeling our best – emotionally, mentally, physically, and spiritually.

Five things are noteworthy about this definition:

Self-care is personal. A self-care plan is based on your unique circumstances. You cannot necessarily use someone else's plan. We can't all use my plan. You can't use a plan you read about in BuzzFeed. Your age, occupation, family composition, community service activities, caretaking responsibilities, and access to resources will determine what self-care is right for you.

Self-care is a daily practice. It is not relegated to the weekends, once a quarter, or at that yearly retreat you attend in the mountains. Self-care has to happen every day because you go through life every day. Letting stress build-up is harmful to the body and mind. You must do something every day that contributes to taking care of yourself. It could be for five minutes or 90 minutes. Just do something.

Self-care leads to increased resilience. The goal is not to eliminate stress because that is impossible. Stressful moments happen every day. It is harder to bounce back when your stress levels are consistently high. It makes it harder to deal with unexpected things because your room for resilience is compromised. Instead of bouncing back, you may start to experience physical symptoms of uncontrolled stress. You do not want that to happen. Instead, you want to increase your ability to bounce back from stressful occurrences. When you practice self-care daily to keep your stress levels low, your mind and body will be familiar with recovering from difficulties.

Self-care feels good. One problem with uncontrolled stress is that it leads to things that do not make you feel good down to the cellular level. Problems include exhaustion, irritability, depression, anxiety, gastrointestinal issues, and cynicism. You accept high-stress levels because of the external praise you receive for being involved in countless activities that make an impact. The praise can trick you into believing that all stress is good. Low levels of stress can be motivating. However, most people are operating under sustained high stress and that has disastrous consequences. When you get serious about self-care, you increase your chances of feeling good.

Self-care is for all areas of your life. Dr. Peggy Swarbrick defines eight dimensions of wellness as emotional, financial, social, spiritual, occupational, physical, intellectual, and environmental. Each year, I focus on two areas for improvement. When I started helping people practice self-care, I received many inquiries about diet and exercise. American culture is weight-obsessed. I quickly learned to be clear that my services are best for helping people who are overwhelmed. The good news is that these skills are transferable to all the dimensions of wellness.

SELF-CARE IS SELF-PRESERVATION
In addition to bell hooks and Ella Baker, it is impossible to write a self-care book and not quote Audre Lorde. Her most famous quote on the subject is:

"Caring for myself is not self-indulgence. It is self-preservation. And that is an act of political warfare."

The media represents self-care as a series of self-indulgent acts, leading to a perception that it is frivolous and trivial. When you believe self-care is nothing more than a treat, it is easy to dismiss it. In her quote, Audre Lorde asks us to re-examine our perception of self-care.

Self-preservation is "the protection of oneself from harm or death, especially regarded as a basic instinct in human beings and animals." Lorde sees self-care as the basic instinct to protect ourselves from harm or death. That does not sound frivolous or trivial. We are trying to preserve our energy, minds, and bodies. If we do not focus on preservation, we start to wear ourselves down to the point of displaying physical symptoms of stress.

Lorde goes on to say that it is an act of political warfare. For Black women, other women of color, women in male-dominated fields, and people who identify as LGBTQIA+, I consider the "isms" political attacks. Homophobia, misogyny, racism, sexism are threatening our self-preservation. The political attacks chip away at our ability to rest and experience peace. When we are not well, those who seek to harm us win. Therefore, self-care as self-preservation is not optional.

PART 2

Introduction to the CARE Framework

Finding balance and well-being can feel daunting when navigating the complexities of modern life. The CARE Framework is designed to guide us through this journey with a structured approach to self-care. This framework encompasses Clarity, Awareness, Reframe, and Embrace — key elements that will help you understand yourself better, manage stress effectively, and cultivate a fulfilling life.

I initially developed this framework to explain how I transformed my life in 90 days. I further refined it during my 6-week group coaching program, From Overwhelm to Overflow. When I began working with individuals, I noticed a strong desire to get serious about self-care but a need for a step-by-step roadmap. Chapters 5-10 provide the essential elements of this program.

In Chapter 5, **"Clarifying Your Wellness Vision,"** you'll explore the factors that shape your feelings about self-care and uncover your values regarding wellness. You'll then be guided through thought-provoking questions to help crystallize your unique vision for a balanced and fulfilling life.

Chapter 6, **"Cultivating Awareness for Wellness,"** is

dedicated to assessing and bringing awareness to your unique stressors. Through a detailed stress inventory, you'll explore the factors contributing to your stress, allowing you to understand and better address your challenges.

Chapter 7, **"Reframing Overwhelm,"** examines the critical challenges of time management, overcoming procrastination, and managing digital overwhelm. In this chapter, you'll learn how to manage your time with intention, reduce digital overwhelm, and create a more balanced, focused life through practical strategies.

Chapter 8, **"Reframing Overworking**," explores the critical steps of recognizing overworking patterns, such as the Good Student Syndrome and the Salary Trap, and introduces practical strategies like setting boundaries and saying no.

Chapter 9, **"Reframing Overcommitment**," shares the three questions to ask to determine whether you should commit or not.

Chapter 10, "**Embracing Self-Care**," emphasizes the importance of fully committing to self-care by creating a personalized plan. You'll learn how to set realistic self-care goals, anticipate obstacles, and ensure consistency in your routine for long-term well-being.

Each chapter includes reflection questions or activities for you to complete. It's best to tackle Chapters 5-10 one at a time, giving yourself a week for each to fully absorb the content. Set aside an hour each week to work through the activities.

Chapter 5
Clarifying Your Wellness Vision

CLARIFYING YOUR INFLUENCES
Many of us were shown only a few paths to success growing up: Entertainment and Education. I quickly gave up on the idea of being a Janet Jackson background dancer and went the education route instead. I also picked up on the signals that educated people do and don't do certain things. One thing I was sure of was that educated people drank wine and went to art museums. Here's the thing — I'm not an art person. There is no art on the walls of my home and I've lived in the same place for over a decade.

But from the outside looking in, one would think I loved art because I always attended art exhibits with friends. Why? Because I thought that's what educated people do.

Out of 14 first cousins, I was the only one to attend college at an elite school and finish in four years. That gave me access to opportunities others didn't have and put me in spaces with people who had no idea what it was like to grow up in the middle of the hood. Now that I was "formally" educated, I thought I had to act the part, trying to fit in with the expectations of this new world. I feared that if I didn't, I might lose everything I had worked for and disappoint my family.

How often do we find ourselves doing things because that's what we think we should do?

That's what good moms do.
That's what good daughters do.
That's what good managers and directors do.
That's what people in this company do.

These are the blueprints we follow without questioning them. Many of us have never taken the time to identify what influences us and if those influences align with what we want.

More specifically, have we considered what influences how we care for ourselves?

Throughout my public health and healthcare career, I've noticed an unwritten list of "SHOULDS" that dictate how we approach self-care in this field.

1. We should work long hours.
2. We should accept low pay.
3. We should work while on vacation.
4. We should say yes to any request.
5. We should work nights and weekends.
6. We should volunteer outside of work.

This list is a recipe for needing more time or money to invest in our wellness, even while trying to positively impact people, programs, and policies in public health.

I realized that nothing in my environment encouraged me to believe that caring for myself was essential or normal. All my examples were people who worked long hours and gave their all to their commitments. At best, I saw that hair, nails, and clothes mattered. But was I being physically fit, going to therapy, and setting boundaries? Those were the things I desperately needed; but how was I to know?

Growing up, I thought I didn't see any examples of self-care. But as I began working to decolonize my mind, I realized that I had seen people taking care of themselves — it just looked different than what I expected. It was community care. My family celebrated holidays and went to church together. We always knew we could pick up the phone and connect. Those relationships were priceless. But what I did not see was how to take care of myself as a Black woman in a white-collar, salaried job — a job that followed me home every day. Whether it was my laptop or a printout, my work always came home.

Taught or Caught?
It's important to understand what's guiding our current behavior before making changes. Many of our ideas about self-care aren't our own; we pick them up along the way. Some things are explicitly taught, while others are caught through observation or social norms. Below are a few questions that can help you uncover what influences your approach to self-care. Take time to reflect on these questions in a quiet space. My coaching clients have shared that these questions can bring up uncomfortable emotions, so please reach out to a therapist or counselor if any of them feel triggering.

What did my family teach me about self-care? What did my community teach me about self-care?

What ideas about self-care did I catch from society?

What ideas about self-care did I catch from my workplace or profession?

CLARIFYING YOUR VALUES

I began writing this book by sharing my career journey. For over a decade, my career was my sole focus. It's where I invested the majority of my time and energy. Why? Because it was what I valued.

In the last section, we explored what influences our self-care, which shapes what we value. Values are "a person's principles or standards of behavior; one's judgment of what is important in life." The part of the definition we're focusing on here is "what is important in life."

If someone asked you what is most important in life, would your answers reflect how you spend your time, money, and energy? For many of us who are career-driven, there's often a disconnect. What we say we value might not coincide with how we live. Bringing work home, checking phones at the dinner table, and working late into the night reflect that we value working hard. While that might be for a good reason, we might also value family time, but somehow, it never gets the same attention as our work.

Before making meaningful changes in your life, you need to understand the values that will guide you. Influences guide you from external sources, but values come from

Clarifying Your Wellness Vision

within. Your values can only be a compass if you know what they are. Decision-making becomes more manageable when you have clear values and are more likely to feel aligned with who you are.

Clarifying your values is a two-step process. The first step is to identify how your values currently appear. Take time to reflect on and answer these questions:

- What were the top three things I spent time on in the last seven days?
- What were the top three things I spent the most discretionary money on in the previous seven days?
- What were the top three things I spent the most time thinking about in the last seven days?
- In the last seven days, outside of work conversations, what were the top three things I spent the most time talking, texting, or posting about on social media?
- What three words would describe how life felt in the last seven days?

Your responses reflect what you currently value. They show up in your actions, even if not intentionally. They may or may not align with what you wish to value. Are these the values you want to live by? If not, take control.

If you need to create or revise your values, you can answer similar questions. This time, let's look toward the future. You can intentionally select values that will guide you moving forward.

- By the end of the year, what will be the top three things I will have invested my time in?
- By the end of the year, what will be the top three things I will have spent the most discretionary money on?
- By the end of the year, what will be the top three things I will have spent the most time thinking about?
- By the end of the year, outside of work conversations, what will be the top three things I will have spent the most time talking, texting, or posting about on social media?
- By the end of the year, choose three words that describe how life will feel most days.

After completing this exercise, you'll have a list of about a dozen values. It's helpful to prioritize up to three that are most important. For example, my top three values are integrity, ease, and grace. These values are my guiding principles in all my actions and decisions.

- **Integrity**: I won't do it if I can't be honest. This applies to both the big and small things. I no longer tell little lies like "I'm on my way" when I'm not even dressed.
- **Ease**: I avoid things that make me feel rushed or pressured. I no longer pack my day with back-to-back tasks. I also set reasonable deadlines for the things I'm working on.
- **Grace**: I assume good intentions and goodwill. Life is hard for everybody, so I do my best to give people the benefit of the doubt.

Clarifying Your Wellness Vision

When we live in alignment with our values, we feel better. Even if it's unintentional, living out of alignment with our values brings suffering. There's internal conflict. I want us all to live better by living out our actual values. The sooner we get in alignment, the better.

CLARIFYING YOUR VISION

One of the reasons you may be drawn to this book as a high-achieving woman is because you desire a different life. The life you're currently living is likely not the one you envisioned. I'm confident no one envisioned trying to fit 75 things into a 24-hour day or having persistent high-stress levels. Nor did you imagine a life without enough time for the people who matter most.

Just like with our influences, what we envision for our lives is often shaped by the standard American vision, which comes from making standard American decisions. Some of these fundamental decisions include education, where we choose to live, our family arrangements, and our career paths. These four essential factors determine much about our lives; most have followed a similar path. Those decisions teach us that work comes first, family comes second, and everything else falls into place afterward. Statistics show that work is one of the main contributors to stress in our lives. When we choose a job, most of us don't consider how stressful it will be. Even if we do, we often accept it as "part of the package". I have not met anyone who said, "I knew the job was stressful, so I proactively managed my stress."

What usually happens is that we reach a point of

overwhelm and start searching for a book like this to figure things out—often when we have the fewest mental, physical, and sometimes financial resources to do so.

Another ordinary reality is that most of us don't have written vision statements for every dimension of our lives. As the health and wellness chair on a neighborhood improvement committee, I co-hosted a Vision Board Party. It was my first time experiencing one. A vision board is a collage of images and words that inspire or motivate us to achieve our goals or desires.

Until then, I had only created a vision for my career—the classic five-year plan. However, everyone completed the "wheel of life" exercise during the Vision Board Party. The Wheel of Life asks us to rate our satisfaction with different areas of our lives on a scale of one to ten. This was the first time I intentionally considered various aspects of my life and it inspired what I chose to include on my vision board.

However, even with that introspection, my vision board still reflected the standard American dream. I had images of a big house, dream vacations, and an expensive car—many material things. What I didn't include were the consequences of striving for those things. Some of them were expensive, and unless I won the lottery, I'd need to change careers or add a second income stream, which would bring more stress. I also missed reflecting on how I wanted my days to *feel*.

The next time I created a vision board, I took a different approach. Instead of jumping straight to the vision board, I first visualized my ideal day and journaled, which allowed me to tap into what I *truly* wanted. After identifying my values and journaling, the vision board I created—one that reflected ease and grace—looked very different from my first one. For instance, I no longer had a large house on my vision board. My current home is 2,000 square feet. That is just enough space for my husband and me, since neither of us actually enjoy cleaning the space we already have. A bigger house is not necessary for my vision of happiness. I want larger closets, but that doesn't require more square footage. I've learned to be content with my vision because it's truly *mine*.

Now that I understand my values better, I know I want freedom and I like it. Every decision I make moves me closer to freedom with integrity, ease, and grace. Some might say having these values simultaneously isn't possible, but I'm living proof that it is. It hasn't been easy and it required discipline, but it's happening. And it's not just happening for me—others who take the steps outlined in this book are also living this reality.

Creating a new vision is often the most challenging part for my clients. We have very few realistic examples of people living with ease and grace. It's a significant departure from the standard American vision built on standard American decisions. But working 40 hours or less in a salaried job is possible while others work 60. It *is* possible to leave work on time every day so you can spend time with your children during daylight hours. It *is* possible to step down from leadership positions without feeling guilty. It *is* possible to leave your work laptops at home while on vacation. And it *is* possible to use every vacation day you've earned.

Your vision is your roadmap. Organizing each piece of your vision allows you to create your desired reality. However, you must commit to one thing to make this vision a reality.

You cannot share your vision with everybody.

When I began working reasonable hours, I didn't make an announcement. I didn't tell anyone that I had stopped working nights and weekends. I just quietly made the change. I ensured all my work was completed by Friday, ensured that I wasn't a bottleneck, and avoided leaving anyone needing after-hours help. And you know what? It worked. No one noticed.

You might be hesitant to try something similar, afraid of what others might say. But what if they don't say anything at all? What if they're too busy overworking themselves to pay attention to you? And even if someone *says* something, you can always correct it. So far, none of my clients have had anyone notice when they started setting boundaries around their work hours.

It takes courage and bravery to be different. You must

remove the "woe is me, I'm working so many hours, praise me" conversations. You can no longer wear overworking as a badge of honor. Once you reclaim your time, you'll have space to do something more fulfilling.

WRITING YOUR WELLNESS VISION
How do you write one if you've never had a personal vision? How do you know what you genuinely want beyond the standard American dream? The key is to align your vision with the values you wish to live out.

When writing your wellness vision, you should use the present tense, as though it's already real and happening. This approach primes you to work on making it a reality. Writing in the future tense can make the vision feel distant as if it's out of reach.

For example, in my vision, I wake up every day and sit on a veranda to pause, reflect, and meditate. I don't have a veranda, but I wake up daily to pause, reflect, and meditate. I live near a park with a creek and go there to reflect. When I visit my in-laws, they have a lovely porch, and I make sure to use it. When renting an Airbnb, I always seek one with a veranda, patio, or outdoor space. We can strive to experience as much of our vision as possible, even before we have every piece in place.

Moreover, when writing your wellness vision, create a positive, inspiring, and affirmative picture of what life will look like when all is well. Your vision should reflect the values you want to live by, starting with the end in mind. Write in the affirmative using statements like *I am, I have,* and *I experience.*

Here's an excerpt from my first wellness vision:

> *I wake up every day without an alarm. I walk to my wellness room, part of the retreat center attached to my home. I light a candle, turn on my aromatherapy machine, grab a cushion, and meditate. After 30 minutes, I go outside onto the porch to journal, read, drink water, and sip tea. Then I walk along the water, stopping to pray and give thanks.*

Creating a wellness vision is a powerful way to prioritize your well-being and set meaningful goals.

Here are 20 journal prompts to help you develop your vision and live with intention.

1. What does wellness mean to you personally? Describe it in detail.

2. Reflect on your current state of well-being. What aspects of your life are thriving and what needs improvement?

3. Imagine yourself five years from now. How do you envision your overall wellness and quality of life?

Clarifying Your Wellness Vision

4. What are your core values when it comes to well-being? How do they align with your vision?

5. Describe your ideal daily routine that promotes wellness. What activities and habits are part of it?

6. What role does physical health play in your wellness vision? How would you like to improve or maintain it?

7. Explore your emotional well-being. What practices or strategies will help you manage stress and foster emotional resilience?

8. Consider your mental health. How do you plan to nurture and prioritize your mental well-being?

9. What relationships contribute positively to your wellness vision? How will you cultivate and maintain them?

10. Reflect on your spiritual well-being. What practices or beliefs support your spiritual growth and inner peace?

11. Think about your career or purpose. How does your work contribute to your overall wellness and how can it better align with your vision?

12. Explore your financial well-being. What financial goals can help you feel more secure and

aligned with your wellness vision?

13. Describe your ideal living environment. How does it support your wellness goals?

14. Consider your social life. What social activities or connections are essential for your well-being?

15. Explore your creative side. How can creativity and self-expression be integrated into your wellness vision?

16. Reflect on your self-care practices. What self-care rituals are essential to you and how will you prioritize them?

17. What role do education and personal growth play in your wellness vision? What skills or knowledge do you want to acquire or enhance?

18. Think about your community involvement. How can giving back and connecting with your community contribute to your well-being?

19. Consider any obstacles or limiting beliefs hindering your wellness vision. How can you overcome them?

20. Write a letter to your future self expressing your commitment to achieving your wellness vision and the steps you'll take to achieve it.

Clarifying Your Wellness Vision

These journal prompts can serve as a foundation for exploring and developing your unique wellness vision, paving the way for a healthier, more fulfilling life.

You don't need to worry about getting it perfect right away. You can revise and refine your vision as many times as you need. Don't be afraid to think big, bold, and unapologetic. This is your chance to create a vision that is uncompromising and ultramodern, reflecting the life you truly desire. Be open to the possibility that something even more significant than what you had imagined could manifest. The key to escaping the cycle of overwhelm, overwork, and overcommitment is to clarify what your ideal life looks and feels like.

This clarity gives you purpose. It motivates you to wake up daily and move closer to making your vision a reality. With this clear direction, you can show up for work consistently—and that consistency will start to show up in your life in even more powerful ways. It also reinforces why you must take self-care seriously.

Remember, it's important not to share the vision with anyone. When you step outside the standard American narrative to pursue something radical, unconventional, and different, others may not always respond enthusiastically or supportably.

By keeping your vision private, you protect it. No one can laugh at it. No one can doubt it. No one can project their fears onto it. People will notice your transformation as you live out your vision. Eventually, they'll ask how you did it—and that's when you can share proof that this kind of life is possible. You'll be living evidence—a testimony of what happens when you commit to your vision and values.

Chapter 6
Cultivating Awareness for Wellness

At the end of my first therapy appointment, the verdict was clear. I lacked awareness. I was lost as to how I ended up with severe anxiety, on six medications, and short-term disability.

I am not the only one. Here's what I heard from my clients:

> "I tend to overlook stress because it doesn't always manifest in how I recognize it. When I say, 'I'm feeling pretty stressed,' my edges have already left the building. I'm improving, but knowing how it shows up, especially when busy, would help with earlier intervention."

> "My biggest challenge with dealing with stress is not recognizing and intervening before I feel overwhelmed by it. I'll keep powering through until it feels too big and then feel helpless about it. I

should employ all the tools I have earlier."

"I deal with anxiety and depression. My biggest issue is feeling like I can't control my emotions of being overwhelmed, worried, and anxious. This, in turn, drains me of energy to do things to manage stress, and when it gets horrible, it impacts my ability to do well in my responsibilities and my relationships."

You are not alone in your lack of awareness. If someone had asked me, I might have blamed the people around me. I know we can't change others and I felt helpless to do anything about it at one point. But with the suggestions in this chapter, I realized that I was doing things that also contributed to my stress—stuff I could work on. That realization empowered me. Let's get into it!

STOP ASSUMING

You may be making assumptions about the sources of your stress. Maybe you're blaming your family or the people you work with. These are just assumptions. You must step back and observe what's happening in your life. When you do that, you might realize your assumptions were off or discover additional factors you hadn't even considered — things that a manicure, pedicure, or Netflix binge won't fix.

I've noticed that many of us are using strategies that won't give us the results we're hoping for. When working 16-hour days, my regular mani-pedis wouldn't help me with my overwhelm. The real solution was taking things off my plate. But that wasn't the advice I was seeing in blogs or magazines. It wasn't until I looked at my situation that I saw results. I officially resigned from several volunteer commitments and being the family mediator. We won't figure these things out by making assumptions. Doing a stress inventory and identifying what's causing our stress is the only way to find the right solutions.

When I did my stress inventory, it opened my eyes to what was going on. I realized that, even before I got to work, I was living in chaos (also known as personal craziness). Most mornings, I couldn't find my keys or my MetroCard for public transportation. Misplacing things made me late and I always rushed to make my first meeting. It may seem like a small thing, but it was happening every day. Without that stress inventory, I wouldn't have realized that misplacing my keys was a significant source of stress, making an already challenging situation even worse.

HOW TO COMPLETE A STRESS INVENTORY
A traditional inventory is a complete list of items like property, goods, or the contents of a space. In the same way, a stress inventory is a complete list of the things that are either increasing or decreasing your stress. Without a stress inventory, you might continue working on assumed things that have nothing to do with what's stressing you out.

A stress inventory should be completed over 24 hours. Every hour, write down the activities you were involved in and note whether that activity increased or decreased your stress. Just like reviewing online banking transactions, where one column is for deposits and the other for withdrawals, you'll log each activity and how it made you feel.

Begin with the moment you wake up. How did you feel? What did you do in those first few hours? Did you focus on basic hygiene and self-care? Did you pick up your phone and scroll through Instagram? Did you check your work email? How did these things make you feel?

Once you begin working, tracking becomes even more essential. Did that weekly meeting with Amber leave you feeling uneasy? Did you take a lunch break? Did Brenda's email spike your blood pressure? Did the updates from your team leave you feeling proud?

After work, continue tracking until bedtime. Did you check emails later? How did you feel while making dinner? Did doing laundry give you a sense of peace or irritate you? What did that unexpected phone call make you think? When did you spend time with family? What time did you go to bed? What activities did you do for meaning and enjoyment?

This process requires focus. It won't work if you just jot down "worked from 9 to 12" because every meeting or task differs. If you had three meetings between 9 and 12, one could be fun with people you enjoy; another could be frustrating with people who irritate you and the third might have had you multitasking, so you weren't fully present. Each situation affects you differently.

It's important to track each activity and evaluate it

carefully. Is this task increasing stress and draining your energy, peace, and focus? Or is it decreasing your stress and replenishing your energy, peace, and focus?

Below is an example of a typical morning when I did this exercise for the first time.

6:00 am - Checked email and started working (anxious)
7:00 am - Continued to work, checked Facebook (anxious and holding breath)
7:30 am - Got ready for work (distracted, wound up about how much I have to do)
8:00 am - Rushing to get out the door and can't find keys, missed the bus (hurried and worried that I wouldn't get to work on time)
9:00 am - Got breakfast tacos (relaxed a bit)

REFLECT ON WHAT YOU LEARNED FROM YOUR INVENTORY

When I looked at my inventory, I noticed a few things:

- Much of my stress is self-induced.
- I want to stop mindless social media surfing.
- Getting out the door on time takes a lot of work.
- I must write things down because I have too many tasks to remember.
- I am in a constant state of panic.
- I can't avoid the "wall of meetings".

It was clear to me what needed to change. Some of these things I wasn't initially aware of. The things I was aware of, I felt powerless to change, so I never tried. At this point,

I had nothing to lose, so I got professional help, took classes, read books, and tried new routines designed for each issue. For example, I read the book, *Getting Things Done*, by David Allen to learn how to manage my list and stay on top of tasks.

Now it's your turn to reflect.

- List the beliefs, routines, and habits that get in the way of you realizing the vision you've set for yourself.
- List the things that routinely make you feel bad or lead to negative stress responses.
- Pick three areas that will be the first steps toward feeling better. At least one of these should be something you can do in the next week.

Finish this sentence: In the next three months, I want to work on _____.

Chapter 7
Reframing Overwhelm

In my experience with working with career-driven women, three recurring challenges are overwhelming, overworking, and overcommitting. Chapters 7-9 invite us to reframe these issues and provide practical strategies for lasting change.

Let's start with understanding overwhelm. Many describe it as accomplishing 75 tasks in a 24-hour day, which is generally impossible. Considering that we sleep five to eight hours, the time left in the day is limited. Therefore, we need to use our available time wisely.

A decade ago, I took on a job to ensure every American could easily access information about HIV policy and programs. I didn't anticipate this would involve managing one of the most extensive communication operations in the federal government. Each day felt like being on a conveyor belt. Tasks were coming so rapidly that I had no time to think, let alone develop a system to manage the overwhelming workload.

AVOID THE BUFFET METHOD OF TASK MANAGEMENT
A common mistake when going to a buffet restaurant is loading your plate with so much food that you end up with more than you can handle. You start down the line, selecting

your favorite items and filling your plate. As it starts to pile up, you spot your absolute favorite dish. What do you do? Do you skip it? No, it's the dish you want most.

Do you take something off your current plate and put it back? No, that would be unsanitary.

Do you grab it and decide to skip some of the other food? No, that would be wasteful.

Do you grab a second plate and try to eat everything? Yes.

Then, you end up feeling stuffed, uncomfortable, and regretful. You might even drop your plate trying to carry it all to the table and create a mess.

This situation is similar to deciding what to take on at work, home, and in the community. You rarely have all our options presented at once. Each task, commitment, or obligation comes individually through emails or conversations. It's easy to forget what you've agreed to, and without a clear visual like a physical plate, you might end up overwhelmed.

For the time you do have, you need to figure out the maximum limit of focus and energy you can dedicate to getting things done. Beyond that, you risk operating in H.O.T. M.E.S.S mode: **Hurried, Overwhelmed, and Tired Makes Every day Super Stressful.**

In this mode, you're inadequate for yourself and the people you care about.

To prevent overwhelm, you need to address the thought patterns contributing to it. One typical pattern is equating a full plate with personal value. A full plate often means a packed schedule, with back-to-back or even double and triple-booked meetings. Your days become draining and there's no time to recharge. A full plate isn't a status symbol; what truly matters is your effectiveness and impact. You can make a meaningful impact without being involved in too many things.

Being overwhelmed is not a part of the new vision you crafted for yourself in Chapter 5. The vision is not something you write once and set aside. Reading your vision daily keeps your desires at the forefront of your mind. As you navigate the buffet of life, you must assess whether your choices are moving you toward or away from that vision. If you do too many things that distract you from your vision, overwhelm can easily creep in.

TIME MANAGEMENT MOTTOS
I cried on the Friday of my first week in my new position and immediately sought solutions, though I didn't fully grasp the extent of my problem. I listened to *Getting Things Done* by David Allen. While the system felt too complex, it helped me recognize some beliefs that kept me in chaos. After reading the book, I wrote a list of new beliefs to help me stay focused and avoid falling back into old patterns. Here are three beliefs I started with:

It is okay to be early. Being late was a significant source of my overwhelm, so I affirmed, "It is okay to be early." Arriving ahead of time is acceptable.

Be a finisher. I realized that procrastination often sneaks in when I might start tasks early. I remind myself to move ahead and complete the task. I used to get 80% done and then take a break, only to rush to finish at the last minute.

My mind is for having ideas rather than for holding them. I used to believe that remembering everything made me wiser. I tried to keep things in my mind instead of writing them down, spending more time worrying about what I might forget than actually doing the tasks. This overload made me feel overwhelmed and unsure of my mind's reliability.

I decided to stop trying to remember everything; it just wasn't working. Now, I document everything on paper or electronically. When I lost my notebook once, I couldn't recall almost anything I needed to do or know. It was scary but also liberating. I felt free from the burden of trying to remember everything. Now, everything is documented.

This also gives me a reference point before making decisions. When asked to do something, I always respond, "Hold on, let me check my notebook." If I answer without checking, it's a guess rather than a thoughtful yes, no, or maybe.

This aligns with what we discussed in Chapter 5. Review the values you wrote down and confirm them daily to guide and hold yourself accountable for the changes you want to make.

TIME MANAGEMENT TOOLS AND SYSTEMS

The next step in avoiding overwhelm is finding the right tools and systems. These tools and systems act as your figurative plates, allowing you to see what you need to work on. It took me a long time to determine which tools and systems worked best. In the next section, we'll explore how to choose tools and systems to help you manage your tasks without feeling overwhelmed.

Reframing Overwhelm

For me, it made sense to use a digital tool integrated with my work systems to manage my tasks and to-do lists. I experimented with numerous apps but never quite figured out how to make them work for me. I resorted to sticky notes, but with the fast pace of the job, I couldn't keep up with all the paper. I'd switch back to digital tools, then try fancy journals with appealing layouts. None of these worked because I hadn't stopped to consider what I needed or analyzed what was wrong with my previous tools.

Even after a year of focusing on self-care, I still didn't have a solid system for managing my tasks and obligations. As a result, I would overcommit and end up feeling overwhelmed again. I was waking up at 4 a.m., anxious about the day ahead. The anxiety was resurfacing and I knew I needed to find something that worked for me.

I reflected on exactly what I needed from a system or tool. I wanted something that would reduce my anxiety, boost my energy, decrease chaos, enhance responsiveness, improve my sleep, and increase my focus. It wasn't about whether the tool was digital or on paper—it was about its effectiveness.

In the end, I chose the Bullet Journal Method. The key here is "method". Although there's now an app and notebook for sale, it originally started as a system that could be used with any blank notebook. Throughout the day, I write everything I need to remember in short bullet points—whether tasks or pieces of information. I meticulously review the list, marking completed items off. If a task remains unfinished, I convert the bullet into an arrow to indicate it will be carried over to the next day. This practice keeps me accountable and ensures I address any unfinished business.

My task list for the next day includes: 1) the following action for tasks completed the previous day, 2) items not completed from the previous day, and 3) new requests from emails, conversations, or calls.

I follow this routine daily until Friday. On Friday, if a task has been on the list all week without any progress, I ask myself: 1) Is this the next action? 2) Can I delegate it? 3) Can I delete it? I strive to avoid letting things linger.

Whether you already have a planner or digital app or are seeking something custom, this checklist (including some criteria that others have found helpful in reducing overwhelm) can help you determine if it's a right fit:

- Flexible layouts or tracking system
- Simple and easy to use
- Space for inspiration
- Clear visibility of tasks
- Helps in confidently saying yes or no to requests
- Used consistently (80% of the time)
- Tasks are getting done
- You feel better when you use it

Use this list as inspiration and customize it to fit your own needs.

DEALING WITH PROCRASTINATION

You might sometimes dread specific tasks on your to-do list, even if they're dutifully recorded in your bullet journals. For instance, you might face tasks you'd rather

Reframing Overwhelm

avoid, like a boring report you must complete. There's a trick that can help you tackle these tasks called the Pomodoro Method.

Here's how it works:

First, select the task that needs to be completed, even if it's not your favorite. It's usually the one staring you right in the face, demanding your attention. Then, set a timer for just 25 minutes. During this time, focus solely on that task and aim to make some progress.

When the timer goes off after 25 minutes, take a short break, about five minutes, to clear your head. The real magic happens when you repeat this cycle three more times, totaling four rounds of 25 minutes each.

Now, here's the cool part: If, after the first 25 minutes, you're still struggling and the task seems overwhelming, give yourself permission to take a break and return to it later. This rule helps prevent frustration. However, you won't even need to use that rule most of the time. Starting with just 25 minutes often helps you get into a flow and things start moving more smoothly than expected.

Interestingly, sometimes you may set aside two hours for a task, only to find that you're already done after the first 25 minutes! This method helps to overcome procrastination and tackle even the most challenging tasks.

After completing those four productive cycles of 25 minutes each, reward yourself with a more extended break, like 30 minutes. It's a little treat for being productive. So, next time you're faced with a task you'd rather avoid, try this method. In just 25-minute chunks, you'll be amazed at how much you can accomplish, even with challenging tasks.

Chapter 8
Reframing Overworking

After my first week of therapy, I realized I created an impossible situation for myself. Alongside my demanding Director position at my 9-5, I juggled four other unpaid roles: President of my professional association chapter, Committee Chair of a young professionals organization, member of a national committee, and Secretary of the board for my local farmer's market.

Overworking looks different for everyone. For some, it might be volunteering for the PTA, serving a sorority, or serving food to seniors. These are all noble and laudable commitments, but are also classic examples of overworking. I'm not talking about the occasional bake sale; I'm referring to holding elected positions or making regular weekly commitments that are essentially part-time jobs.

You and I both ended up in this position because of three reasons, but I've found solutions to help you overcome these challenges, just like I did.

Good Student Syndrome. I've always been at the top of my class. I could read well by age four, so I skipped Kindergarten. Early on, I noticed that my family's most financially successful people were also the most educated. I calculated that getting a good education was the easiest path to living the American dream. Higher education became increasingly important to me, growing up significantly amidst the gangs and crack epidemic that plagued South Central Los Angeles in the 1980s and 90s.

I set my sights on a college degree. Even though I had a strong interest in the arts, focusing solely on academics was the best way to get into the top colleges. I consistently made decisions that would give me the best chance at staying on top, which always included taking on extracurricular activities to supplement my grades. This approach often got me picked for additional opportunities, but it also meant I didn't make as much time for fun as many of my peers. I was in a rush to grow up.

Good Student Syndrome is about more than just good grades—it's about concern with external expectations, being helpful, not being disruptive, and earning the praise of those in power. It's different from perfectionism because we care more about meeting others' expectations than being the best. Perfectionists need to excel; good students just need to be good.

This mentality likely played a significant role in my success but also led to burnout. It became a lifelong pattern for me—I could never just do one thing at a time. I'm guessing it's similar for you. This ingrained "good student" mindset carries over into adulthood, often resulting in overworking.

As we move into more senior roles, we take on greater responsibilities, and our jobs become more complex. Instead of applying the lessons learned from various opportunities, we often hold onto roles we no longer need. We've arrived at the point we wanted, but our actions still reflect the drive to be the "good student" we've always been.

By now, we have plenty on our résumés and our networks are solid. Those professional, extracurricular activities are no longer necessary for the next opportunity. While our egos love the titles and accolades, our souls crave rest and a return to the childhood joys we left behind. It's time to leave some unpaid labor jobs behind and create space for someone else who is still in the striving phase.

To solve this, I compared the value of my unpaid volunteer roles to my current life and career goals. I realized those roles had outlived their purpose. I resigned from all but one. And you know what? All those organizations are still thriving. Their success wasn't tied to me like I once believed.

The Salary Trap. I come from a working-class background where everyone had those good government 9-5 jobs. When the office was closed, work was done—no after-hours hustle.

When I got my first job after college with a salary and good benefits, my workplace never really closed. The expectation was clear: there would be weeks when we worked well over 40 hours. That was most weeks. We'd be in at 9 a.m. and often not off until 11 p.m., with the occasional Sunday thrown in. Back then, I was proud of that—having a "good" white-collar job felt like an accomplishment.

I worked more than 40 hours at my primary job, doing everything possible to be a "good student" and position myself for graduate school or other career advancements.

This was a crucial ingredient in the recipe for burnout. After returning to work from short-term disability, I became keenly aware that time and energy are finite resources. I could no longer let my employer have unfettered access to my time.

To solve this, I had to determine my limits. It's impossible to know when boundaries have been crossed without defined boundaries.

I started by deciding how many hours I would give to

my employer instead of letting them dictate how much of my time they could take. There are only 168 hours in a week and I had to be deliberate about how to use them. I made a list of the major categories in my life in order of importance and assigned each a time value:

Sleeping: 56 hours
Hygiene: 10 hours
Self-care: 10 hours
Cooking/Cleaning: 8 hours
Personal Relationships: 10 hours
Entertainment: 6 hours
Business: 10 hours
Commuting: 10 hours
Working: 48 hours

My "work hours" limit became 48 hours per week. I started declining any requests that regularly pushed me beyond that number. I didn't announce this to anyone. I simply set the boundary for myself and began taking things off my plate until I consistently stayed within that limit.

It wasn't easy at first. I had to curb my natural enthusiasm for volunteering and doing extra work. I was initially afraid to set this boundary because everyone around me worked hard. However, I had already experienced the consequences of being unable to function in other parts of life due to working too many hours. Without limits, things just aren't sustainable.

I decided to try it, figuring I could adjust if anyone raised concerns about my performance or output. But that never happened. Instead, I became more efficient with my time because I was committed to my wellness. Setting these limits allowed me to show up fully without burnout. As a result, I continued to be a quality contributor and the raises and promotions followed more easily.

We should determine how we want to spend the 168 hours per week, including determining the limit on the hours we will work for our employer(s).

No Ain't In Your Vocabulary. A typical advice is, "No is a complete sentence." When I first heard this, it struck me that even though I had an extensive vocabulary, "no" was a word I rarely used.

Some people embrace this advice with ease. But for many of us, including most of my coaching clients, saying "no" doesn't come naturally. As Good Students, we weren't taught to say no or use its variants. While it's true that we don't owe anyone an explanation, I've found that having some go-to phrases makes it easier for us to express that boundary when needed.

<u>Ways to Say No Without Saying No</u>
- I'd love to, but I'm overcommitted right now.

Reframing Overworking

- I'm not taking on any new projects right now.
- That's not my thing, but thanks for thinking of me.
- I can't this week, but please let me know if you have flexibility.
- Accepting this would take me over my limits.

Sometimes, the answer might be "yes," but we just need a different time frame. In these situations, we must set our boundaries around when the request will be completed. Here are some responses to consider:

- I am available to work on this at _____.
- I'm reviewing this document for two hours on Thursday from 3-5 pm.
- I will get back to you by…..
- I don't check email after 7:00 pm. If you have an urgent need, please text me.

Recognizing and addressing the factors contributing to overworking is crucial to achieving a healthier work-life balance. The Good Student Syndrome, driven by external expectations and a desire to excel, can lead us into a pattern of feeling overwhelmed. Similarly, the Salary Trap, where a demanding job becomes a constant presence in our lives, often fuels burnout. Learning to say no, setting clear boundaries, and evaluating the value of our commitments are vital strategies to help us avoid overworking. By prioritizing our well-being and intentionally managing our time, we can break free from the cycle of overworking and create a more sustainable, fulfilling professional and personal life. Saying no can empower us to focus on what truly matters and enhance our overall effectiveness and happiness.

Chapter 9
How to Avoid Overcommitment

Making and keeping commitments to ourselves is a cornerstone of personal growth and fulfillment. The most considerable cost of failing to honor these commitments is the disappointment we inflict on our spirit. When we repeatedly break promises to ourselves, we erode self-trust, which can have far-reaching consequences for our self-esteem and overall well-being.

External demands do not usually pose the most significant challenge, but rather when our inner commitment to our goals, dreams, and self-care is often neglected. Over time, the habit of overcommitting to others at the expense of our wellness can lead to self-neglect. We wake up one day, realizing that we've crowded out our own health and self-care routines, and this realization can be profoundly disheartening.

The good news, however, is that we can change this pattern.

During the height of the COVID-19 pandemic, I found myself helping healthcare systems transform their operations. I also had to transform how I delivered my highly interactive services into virtual formats. A colleague approached me about working with an organization on their strategic plan and I was excited. It was a chance to see if my talents could have the same impact virtually. I thought I was asked to help facilitate the virtual meeting, so I mentally calculated the time, and agreed.

After the first meeting, I started sensing that I may have unknowingly agreed to more than I realized. Finally, I asked a question I should have asked from the start: "How much time did you budget for me on this project?" She replied, "12 days." This project lasted over 6-8 weeks—nearly 100 hours of work! I couldn't absorb that without overworking. At that moment, I realized I had overcommitted.

I felt balanced when this opportunity was presented—something I hadn't felt often. It was pleasant but unfamiliar. I sensed I had room to do more and my natural inclination was to fill that space. But less than 15 minutes later, I had somehow agreed to 100 extra hours of work. The more appropriate response to feeling like I had more bandwidth would've been to protect that feeling at all costs. It wasn't what I was used to but what I truly desired.

I stuck it out, but I immediately started planning to avoid this. Below are three questions that helped during my planning which I suggest you answer before committing to something.

1. **Can you send me the plan?** If someone can't produce a plan or provide details, the answer is automatically no. They don't know what they're asking you to commit to. You can ask them to come back when they have more information. If they do have a plan, you should review it. Based on your experience, you should be able to estimate the time required to execute and identify gaps.

    Next, check your digital calendar or paper planner to assess the available time. When could you realistically fulfill the project's requirements? Will you be able to stay balanced? If fitting it in means working nights and weekends, it might be time to consider declining.

2. **Is this a hell yes?** If you're still unsure after asking the first set of questions, it's time to turn inward and question yourself. Are you also saying yes to your needs and priorities while agreeing to this request? We've all been in situations where we've said yes out of obligation, only to complain about it later—especially for things that weren't even required but we took on anyway. That's a sign we weren't aligned with what truly mattered to us. Another way to reflect on this is by asking, "How will this benefit my overall vision for my life?"

   Return to the example above where I was asked to help with virtual strategic planning. Usually, I wouldn't have been as excited. I've done strategic planning successfully many times before, so it wouldn't have added anything new to my resume. However, in that specific context, it felt aligned because it presented a novel challenge, allowed me to build my network, and provided testimonials for my work.

   But I didn't consider everything. I would need to work nights and weekends. Was this opportunity worth sacrificing rest or cutting into personal time? In hindsight, it wasn't. I worked on it every night and weekend and thought, "Why did I agree to this?"

   The answer to whether this was a "hell yes" was mixed, and in reality, that means it wasn't one.

3. **Will declining be detrimental?** Let's just have some real talk for a second. You find yourself overcommitted because you fear the consequences of saying no. "Detrimental" means something that causes harm, damage, or adverse effects. In your view, something is detrimental if it could lead to severe outcomes—like

dying, getting fired, or hurting someone. With that in mind, many things you fear, like people being disappointed or not wanting to work with you anymore, aren't genuinely detrimental.

You often assume serious consequences out of fear, but there may be little to no adverse outcomes from saying no. In many instances, you have unconsciously become "the dependable one". It's not that others can't come through, but people rely on you because you've always said yes. Some have even developed bad planning habits, knowing you'll swoop in and save the day at the last minute. While this might feel efficient for them, it leaves you overburdened.

When your yes becomes less dependable, a few things may happen. The person will find someone else, often without thinking any less of you. If they seem upset, it's not about you—they're just annoyed they now have to spend more time finding someone to meet their needs. It's not personal. When you decline specific opportunities, you make space for others. There's always someone else out there who could benefit from the opportunity more than you would.

Going through this process brings real benefits. The more intentional you are with your time, the more you'll see positive outcomes.

Remember, avoiding overcommitment is about keeping commitments to yourself. It's not just about hitting specific goals—it's about honoring your worth and nurturing your self-respect. When you prioritize yourself and follow through on promises you make to yourself, you'll discover a renewed sense of purpose, fulfillment, and a deeper connection to your true aspirations. Take a vow to wake up each day to honor your commitments and watch your self-esteem and personal growth soar to new heights.

Chapter 10
How to Embrace Self-Care

In this book, I present the CARE Framework, not a formula, because everyone is different. Nothing we've discussed in this book is meaningful until you put it into daily practice. When I started this journey, my goals were simple: 1) Do whatever I needed to do to make it to the next therapy appointment, and 2) Go to work and stay there all day. With those two goals in mind, I experimented with different self-care practices to help me achieve them. You have to do the same. You're much more likely to see actual results when you embrace self-care.

HOW DO YOU FIND TIME FOR SELF-CARE?
The best time for self-care is now. It's time to create a schedule reflecting your true priorities. Your digital or paper calendars often capture the activities where you show high commitment. Your self-care activities are just as crucial as work meetings and other obligations—they deserve a place on your calendar alongside everything else you've chosen to commit to. When you embrace self-care as a daily practice rather than an occasional indulgence, you intentionally create the time for it.

Let's start from scratch. Open a blank weekly calendar page or print one. First, mark off time for sleep, then block out time for self-care. Once that's done, you'll see how much time is left for everything else. Those who are serious about self-care don't sacrifice it for other commitments. If your other obligations don't fit, something has to give if you want to stop feeling overworked, overwhelmed, and overcommitted.

As we've discussed, doing something different from what everyone else is doing can initially feel uncomfortable. But you must push through that discomfort to get what you want. You must stay committed to achieving the vision you've outlined for yourself. You must make the time.

Believe it or not, you already have the time. I've never worked with anyone who wasn't doing something for their self-care. It's not always about adding new activities. Let's identify the self-care practices already working for you and commit to them more fully. You must ensure those practices are on your calendar, just like anything else. You likely found time already set aside for self-care in the stress inventory and the 168-hour schedule you completed earlier. You may simply need to adjust what you do during that time to better align with your current self-care goals.

CREATING YOUR SELF-CARE PLAN

This is where everything comes together. Let's start by revisiting the definition of self-care:

"Self-care is a set of personal practices that build our resilience and support us in feeling our best—emotionally, mentally, physically, and spiritually."

Now, it's time to determine the activities you need on a daily, weekly, or monthly basis to build that resilience and support your well-being. If you've followed the process in this book, you should already have a clear sense of the areas that need attention. The questions below will help you summarize what you've learned and identify where to focus your efforts.

1. Review your self-care activities and determine if they serve a purpose or solve a problem. Is more time needed?
2. Review the 1-2 areas of the wellness dimensions where you want more satisfaction. Research activities that can help you achieve this.
3. What signs of stress on the body do you want to tend to?
4. What areas of personal chaos do you want to solve?
5. Based on your stress inventory, are you overdrawn? What withdrawals can you stop? Where do you need more deposits?
6. What are things you can do to avoid being overwhelmed? How can you avoid procrastination?
7. How can you manage your digital overwhelm?
8. What are things you can do to avoid overworking?
9. What are things you can do to avoid overcommitting?

Answering these questions may give you a long list of things to address, which can feel overwhelming. However, you need to narrow it down to get started. The following sections will help make the process more manageable.

PRIORITIZING YOUR SELF-CARE ACTIVITIES

Overcommitting to self-care activities isn't sustainable and can lead to overwhelm. To avoid this, let's take the list you made based on the nine questions above and separate it into the following categories:

1: Easy to change and will be life-changing	3: Easy to change and creates a small change
2: Difficult to change and will be life-changing	4: Difficult to change and creates a small change

For the first 3-6 months, we'll focus on the items in the first box. This approach gives you a better chance for success since these tasks require less effort but will significantly impact your life. Then, we can move on to the rest of the list. As long as you stay committed, you'll see continuous progress.

CREATE A PURPOSEFUL MORNING ROUTINE

How you start your day dramatically impacts how the rest of the day unfolds. The morning is also when most of us have the most control over our time. Once we begin interacting with others, that control lessens. Therefore, your morning routine becomes a space to create order and set the tone for yourself.

When I began my journey, my inventory showed that my mornings were one of the most stressful parts of my day. I could never find my keys, I wasn't walking the dog, and I was grabbing unhealthy breakfast foods. There was a lot of room for improvement, so my morning routine became more intentional and structured.

The activities in my morning routine weren't random things I picked up from a blog. Each task served a specific purpose, making it easier to stick with the routine. The critical question you should ask yourself when creating your morning routine is, "What does my mind, body, and soul need to have a successful day?"

This was my first answer:

How to Embrace Self-Care

Aisha's First Morning Routine

Activity	Minutes	Purpose
Journaling	30	To contain the rumination and anxiety
Yoga	20	To feel grounded enough to leave the house
Breakfast	10	To eat something healthy and not make me nauseous
Tidying (Laundry or Dishes)	10	To create more order in my home
Dog Walking	20	To generate more order in my home and give my dog the attention he deserved
Getting Dressed	30	To give me adequate time to get ready

Tending to your mind, body, and soul first thing in the morning is non-negotiable. Most days, you likely follow a predetermined routine, but there is room for flexibility. When you wake up and ask yourself, "What do my mind, body, and soul need to have a successful day?", the answer might lead you to add an activity or adjust the duration of something already on your list. What remains consistent is that you dedicate time to your morning routine, contributing to feeling successful before 9 a.m. Your day doesn't start with your job; it starts with you.

When committing to self-care, creating a purposeful morning routine is pivotal. Meticulously identify what can be done in the morning to set the stage for a successful day and make these practices non-negotiable. The total time is less important than the intention to nurture your mind, body, and soul. Most other things can wait.

CREATE A STRONG SUPPORT SYSTEM

Barack Obama once said, "Don't be afraid to ask questions. Don't be afraid to ask for help when you need it. I do that every day."

I frequently get the question: "How do I create that strong support system?" Many of my clients say they support everyone else, but when they need support, no one is there for them. That makes it harder for them to stick with their self-care plans. I recommend the following four strategies to help you create a robust support system.

1. **Be open and receptive to receiving help.** Sometimes, you have the people around you but resist letting them help. You might reflexively say, "No, I've got it." Start saying yes, even for small things like letting someone help put a bag in the plane's overhead compartment. Make "yes" your default. You enjoy being helpful to others, but by always saying no, you take away the chance for someone to enjoy being useful to you.
2. **Pay attention to who is showing up.** You assume certain people should be in your support system, like a long-time friend or a close family member. If you feel let down when they don't show up, it's important not to dwell on their absence. Instead, focus on those who

are showing up now and express gratitude. It could be someone you met recently who has been genuinely supportive. They might not have been in your life long, but if they've shown up for you, they are part of your support system.

Also, pray for those who cannot show up. Don't get angry if a family member or friend you expected to be there isn't. Instead, pray for them. They might not be showing up because they are depleted themselves. They might struggle to support you while managing their own challenges. Pray they find the strength to help themselves and build a robust support system as well. If, on the other hand, someone is not showing up for selfish reasons, still pray for them.
3. **Seek out community and professional help.** Some challenges are too heavy for non-professionals to handle. I found community support at church and the yoga studio and professional help from a therapist. These outlets provide valuable support and allow me to discuss progress and positive experiences rather than just focusing on problems.

Creating a comprehensive self-care plan involves combining the insights and strategies discussed here into a personalized, actionable plan. By integrating these steps, you can develop a holistic self-care plan that meets your unique needs, fosters resilience, and supports overall well-being. Consistency and adaptability are critical to reduce overwhelm, overworking, and overcommitting.

WHAT HAPPENS WHEN YOU BECOME SERIOUS ABOUT SELF-CARE?

Congratulations! You are now well on your way. What I'm suggesting would be easy if everyone else was doing it. You will receive both positive and negative feedback. Some people will notice you are less stressed. Other people may call you selfish. It might be easy to let others' negative opinions get you down.

Early on, I faced several guilt trips and created a resource to help. Inspired by James Altucher's "The No Bill of Rights," I developed the "Self-Care Bill of Rights" as a reminder that self-care is not selfish.

Self-Care Bill of Rights

I have the right to:

Put my mental, physical, emotional, and spiritual health above everything and everyone else.
Put self-love into action.
Give to others and the world in a way that energizes me.
Make decisions about my time without guilt.
Adequate sleep.
Pamper myself.
Focus on my physical body and outward appearance.
Define leadership and success in a way that supports self-love in action.
Develop new habits that support self-care.
Speak the truth in all situations.

I read this frequently and it helps me avoid becoming discouraged. It might feel like a lot of work at the beginning of this journey you will soon embark upon. You will be tempted to revert to old habits because they are automatic. Unfortunately, you might find yourself right back in the situation that led you to pick up this book in the first place.

At this moment, you stand at the threshold of a profound transformation. Embracing self-care is not merely a choice; it is a revolution. When facing challenges, hold tight to the vision of a life where your well-being takes precedence. Reclaim autonomy over your time, health, and happiness with each intentional step. Embrace this journey with courage, for it is through self-care that you unlock the door to a future where you survive and thrive.

Thank You to My Pre-Order Supporters!

Khadijah Tribble
Marijuana Policy Trust
www.marijuanapolicytrust.org

Consuela Harris

Cassandra Chess

Deanna Kepka

Allison Tillman

Cheryl Roberts

Kristal Vardaman

Aziza Jones

Attricia Stroupe

Jocelyn Stroupe

Michele Graves

Rashon Graves

Lisa Fitzpatrick

Kyna Thomas

Stephanie Holley

Trina Stroupe

How to Embrace Self-Care

Nicole Thompson

Akiesha Brown-Aaron

Sandra Aispuro

Allison Myers

Aisha Littlejohn

Tabitha Mason-Elliott

Melanie Snyder

Quanisha Green

Tyisana Jones
It's A.Y.A.

Marlin Chinchilla

Christy Hughes

Nakeisha Jones

Emilola Abayomi

Eddie Wiley

Brent Hughes

Mindy Nichamin

Michelle Byrd

Jean Udo

Tajan Renderos
Tajan Renderos Coaching
https://www.tajanrenderos.com/

Krystal Reddick
Total Life Care Coaching
https://www.totallifecarecoaching.com/

Katrina Williams
The Katrina Williams Group, LLC
https://www.katrinawilliams.org/

www.ingramcontent.com/pod-product-compliance
Lightning Source LLC
Chambersburg PA
CBHW050915160426
43194CB00011B/2422